CHAPTERS IN HISTORY

Why Is the White House White?

And Other Questions About Our Presidents' Home

by Peter and Connie Roop

SCHOLASTIC INC.
New York Toronto London Auckland Sydney
Mexico City New Delhi Hong Kong Buenos Aires

Especially for DeLila—The First Lady of Our Hearts!
—C. R. and P. R.

ISBN-13: 978-0-545-07074-4
ISBN-10: 0-545-07074-0

Text copyright © 2009 by Peter and Connie Roop
Illustrations copyright © 2009 by Scholastic Inc.

12 11 10 9 8 7 6 5 4 3 2 1   9 10 11 12 13 14/0
Printed in the U.S.A.
First printing, January 2009

Contents

Why Is the White House White? 1

How Has the White House Changed? 8

What Does the White House
Look Like Today? 13

Which President Got Stuck
in His Bathtub? 17

Which First Lady Hung Laundry
to Dry in the East Room? 22

Who Played Hide-and-Seek
with the President? 28

What Pets Have Lived in the
White House? 34

What Celebrations Are Held
in the White House? 39

CHAPTER 1

Why Is the White House White?

The White House is the home of the president of the United States. It also serves as the president's office. Guests are invited to the White House for special meetings and celebrations. The White House has become a symbol of America all around the world.

But why is the White House white? Let's find out.

First and Second Capitals

George Washington became the first president of the United States in 1789. President Washington moved to New York City, which had been the capital of the United States since 1785.

In 1790, Philadelphia was named the national capital. The Washingtons moved to Philadelphia and lived in a red brick mansion on Market Street.

Many people thought Philadelphia was a good choice for the capital. However, President Washington and Congress decided that the United States government needed a city of its own. But where should the capital of the United States be?

A Capital Is Chosen

President Washington found a place he liked along the Potomac River. There were tall trees and wide fields. There were bears, deer, and ducks.

Congress bought ten square miles of this beautiful land from Maryland and Virginia. They decided to build a new city there. Finally, the United States government would have a home.

Congress named the newly created city Washington and named the area Columbia in honor of Christopher Columbus. It is a special place because it is not part of any state. Today we call our capital Washington, D.C.

FACT: D.C. stands for District of Columbia.

A White House Contest

A contest was held to see who would design the house for the president. The winner would get $500 cash or a medal worth $500.

An Irish-born architect from South Carolina, James Hoban, was picked as the winner. Hoban received the $500 medal.

The president's new home was first called the President's Palace. But that name sounded too much like a king's home. So it was just known as the President's House.

The White House Is Built

The cornerstone for the President's House was laid on October 13, 1792. A cornerstone is a special stone placed at a corner when a building is built.

FACT: This cornerstone is still there, but no one knows exactly where it is!

The workmen building the President's House used sandstone to build the walls. Sandstone is very soft and crumbles easily in freezing temperatures. To protect the

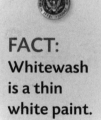

FACT:
Whitewash is a thin white paint.

stone, the walls were covered with whitewash. Eventually white paint was used instead of whitewash. It protected the walls very well.

The White House Gets Its Name

The President's House was white, but it was still called the President's House. Many of the homes during this time were made of red brick. People began to use "White House" as a nickname when they were talking about the President's House. In 1901 President Teddy Roosevelt made the White House the official name. Since then the president's home has been called the White House.

FACT: Today it takes 570 gallons of paint to paint the White House white.

FACT: The nickname "White House" was used as early as 1811.

CHAPTER 2

How Has the White House Changed?

In 1792 James Hoban drew the plans for the President's House. It would be two stories tall. It would have 32 rooms and a basement. At that time, it was a very big house. But there have been many changes made to the White House in the two hundred years since it was built.

President Adams Moves into the President's House

By the time the President's House was finished, George Washington was not president anymore. He was the only president who did not live in the White House.

The builders worked hard to finish the White House. But many rooms were not finished when our second president, John Adams, moved there in November 1800. Only six rooms were complete, and the whole house was wet and damp inside!

The First White House Had No Bathrooms!

In 1800 the White House had no bathrooms. Toilets, called outdoor privies, were outside the White House. The main staircase and the outer steps weren't complete. The Adamses had to enter the house by climbing

temporary wooden steps
and a platform. There were
no closets. The president's
family hung their clothes
in wardrobes. There was no
running water. Water had

to be carried from a spring in a park about five
blocks away.

Still, the Adamses began decorating
the house in an elegant style. They bought
furniture and painted the walls. The next
two presidents, Thomas Jefferson and James
Madison, and their families, continued to
decorate and expand the White House.

Over the years the White House became
a grand home, suitable for our nation's leader.

The White House Burns!

In 1812 the United States was at war with the British. James Madison was president at that time. He left Washington to help the American army.

In 1814, British soldiers attacked Washington and set the White House on fire!

FACT: Before the soldiers set the fire, they helped themselves to a meal in the dining room!

Luckily, a summer thunderstorm put out the fire before it burned to the ground. Most of the White House was ruined. Only the white walls still stood. But they had turned black from the smoke!

It took three years to rebuild the White House. The entire interior had to be built again. All of the rooms were redecorated. And of course, it was given a fresh coat of white paint!

CHAPTER 3

What Does the White House Look Like Today?

Today the White House looks very
different from what it looked like in 1800.
It is much bigger than when it was first built.
A whole wing was added to hold the executive
offices. Front and back
porches were built.
Today the White House
has 132 rooms and six
levels. It has thirty-five
bathrooms and three
elevators!

FACT: President Truman had the insides of the White House torn out and redesigned.

President Theodore
Roosevelt added tennis courts. Franklin
Roosevelt built an indoor swimming pool.

President Nixon added a one-lane bowling alley. Today the White House has a movie theater, basketball court, outdoor pool, and jogging track.

The Rooms of the White House

The White House rooms are different shapes, sizes, and colors. Some are small. Some are large. Some are square. Some are rectangular. Four rooms are shaped like ovals!

FACT: The White House library has 2,700 books.

Many of the rooms are named after colors. The Green Room has been a bedroom, a dining room, a card room, and a sitting room. Since 1800 the president has greeted guests in the Blue Room. The Red Room has been a parlor and sitting room and is sometimes used for small dinner parties.

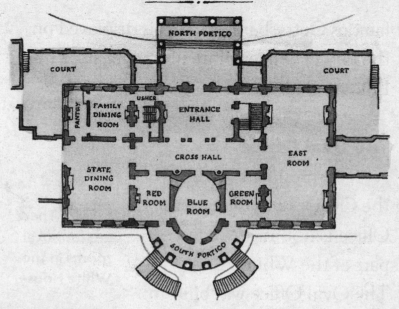

Family Rooms

The presidents and their families live
on the second and third floors of the White
House. There are sixteen bedrooms and
fifteen bathrooms for family and friends to use.
Sometimes friends visiting the president sleep
in the famous Lincoln Bedroom. The Lincoln
Bedroom is like a small Lincoln museum. It has
some furniture used when Abraham Lincoln
was president. A handwritten copy of Lincoln's

famous Gettysburg Address is displayed on the desk. President Lincoln never slept in the Lincoln Bedroom. He used it as an office.

The Oval Office

The president works in the Oval Office. The Oval Office is not in the oldest part of the White House. The Oval Office was built in 1909 in the West Wing of the White House. President Taft was the first president to use the Oval Office. In 1934 it was moved to its present location, overlooking the Rose Garden.

FACT: There are four oval rooms in the White House.

CHAPTER 4

Which President Got Stuck in His Bathtub?

The president of the United States is very busy. But each president finds time to relax. Some presidents played golf or skied. Others went hunting or fishing. Some painted, cooked, played musical instruments, rode horses, or collected stamps. Sometimes silly things happened to presidents.

FACT: President Ford accidentally locked himself out one night when walking his dog.

Stuck in His Tub

President William
Taft was a very large man.
He weighed 332 pounds
and was our heaviest
president. President Taft
liked sports. He was the
first president to play golf.
He danced. He played
tennis. President Taft's

FACT:
President Taft
began the tradition
of the president
throwing the first
pitch to begin each
baseball season.

favorite sport to watch was baseball.

After exercising one day, President Taft climbed into his bathtub. But he was so big, he got stuck! After that, a new bathtub was ordered just for him. President Taft's new tub was big enough to hold four men!

Teddy Roosevelt's Teddy Bear

One day President Teddy Roosevelt was hunting. He saw a bear all by itself. President Roosevelt decided not to shoot the bear.

A man drew a cartoon of President Roosevelt saving the bear's life. In the cartoon, the bear looked like a small cub. A toymaker saw the cartoon. He made a stuffed

baby bear. He sent his bear cub to President Roosevelt. The toymaker asked President Teddy Roosevelt if he could name his bear "Teddy" in his honor.

President Roosevelt said yes. And that is why you might have a "teddy bear" today.

Other Presidential Pastimes

There are lots of interesting stories about our presidents. John Quincy Adams used to wake up two hours before sunrise to go skinny-dipping in the Potomac River. President Grant was arrested for speeding through Washington in his horse and buggy. He had to pay a $20 fine and walk back to the White House. President Teddy Roosevelt liked to greet his supporters. He once shook the hands of 8,513 people in a single day.

President Dwight Eisenhower liked golf so much that he added a putting green to the White House lawn. He was also the first president to be on color TV. President Richard Nixon opened the White House for neighborhood children on Halloween. President Clinton played the saxophone. Do you wonder what will be special about our next president?

CHAPTER 5

Which First Lady Hung Laundry to Dry in the East Room?

Most presidents have been married. The president's wife is called the first lady. Each first lady has added her own touch to life in the White House.

FACT: First ladies have been called "Mrs. President," "Lady," or "Lady Presidentress."

The President's Laundry

Abigail Adams was the first first lady to live in the White House. Her husband, John Adams, was our second president.

Abigail Adams moved into the White House before all the rooms were finished. She hung her laundry to dry in one large room. Today this room is the famous East Room where guests from around the world meet the president and first lady. Hopefully, there is no laundry hanging there now!

FACT: The East Room is the largest room in the White House.

Dolley Madison to the Rescue!

James Madison was the president when the British attacked Washington, D.C. in 1814. First Lady Dolley Madison worried that the White House might be in danger. She knew that there were many valuable things

in the White House, so she worked quickly to save what she could. When the British set fire to the White House, many valuables were safe. One of the things that Dolley saved was a life-size picture of George Washington. Today the picture proudly hangs in the East Room.

Busy Eleanor Roosevelt

Eleanor Roosevelt lived in the White House longer than any other president's wife. She was first lady for more than twelve years. And she was busy all the time!

President Franklin Roosevelt had trouble walking as a result of polio and was often in a wheelchair. Franklin called Eleanor his "eyes and ears" as she traveled around America. Eleanor worked hard for the rights and needs of the poor and minorities.

FACT: President Truman gave Eleanor Roosevelt the nickname "The First Lady of the World."

Eleanor's role as first lady ended when President Roosevelt died in 1945. But she continued working hard to make life better for people everywhere.

Jackie Kennedy's Collections

There are many beautiful and valuable things in the White House. Many are gifts from Americans as well as from friends around the world.

First Lady Jackie Kennedy decided that the White House should proudly display many of these pictures, dishes, furniture, silver, and art. She had pictures hung throughout the hallways. She had special furniture placed in many rooms. She had dishes and silver put out so people could enjoy them. Today, thanks to First Lady Jackie Kennedy, White House visitors see these beautiful things.

FACT: Jackie Kennedy invited many authors, scientists, artists, and musicians to the White House.

CHAPTER 6

Who Played Hide-and-Seek with the President?

Many children have lived in the White House. The White House was their home while their fathers were president. The first children had friends

FACT: Alice Roosevelt loved to slide down the White House stairs on a cookie sheet.

over for birthday parties and sleepovers. They played in the White House. They played outside in the beautiful White House gardens. Living in the White House was a special experience for the first children.

Hide-and-Seek and a Pony Ride

"I don't think that any family has ever enjoyed the White House more than we have," President Teddy Roosevelt said. And they did! The six Roosevelt children played with their pets, tricked guests, and roughhoused with their father.

Every day at four o'clock President Roosevelt stopped what he was doing and played with his children. They played hide-and-seek. They wrestled. They had pillow fights. President Roosevelt told tales of his many adventures in the Wild West.

One day young Archie Roosevelt was sick. He missed his pony, Algonquin. Archie's brother Quentin decided to surprise him by bringing Algonquin up in the White House elevator to see him!

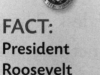

FACT: President Roosevelt always wanted to be "it" when they played hide-and-seek.

Playing in the Oval Office

Caroline and John Kennedy Jr. were young children when they moved into the White House in 1961. Caroline was three years old, and John was two months old!

FACT: John Jr.'s nickname was John-John.

John and Caroline enjoyed being in the Oval Office while their father, President John F. Kennedy, worked. Once Caroline brought her pony Macaroni into the Oval Office!

President Kennedy's wooden desk was very big. The desk was made out of wood from a famous ship. John-John loved to hide under the desk. The front of the desk swung open. Sometimes John-John would open the little door and peek out at people who were meeting with his father.

Growing Up at the White House

Tad Lincoln often dressed as a soldier while he lived in the White House during the Civil War. Tad marched with the soldiers. Tad also sold lemonade to thirsty White House guests.

Amy, President Jimmy Carter's daughter, moved into the White House in 1977. She went to third grade at a public school in Washington. Amy had no trouble with her homework. She could pick from the 2,700

FACT: Amy Carter was known for reading books during state dinners.

books in the White House library! President Carter designed a tree house for Amy in the White House garden. It was bolted together so it wouldn't hurt the tree!

Many presidents had their grandchildren visit the White House. Some grandchildren even lived in the White House. They built snowmen together. They celebrated birthdays, watched movies, swam, and played games together. There is even a special place in the Children's Garden at the White House. It is a paved walkway with handprints and footprints of first children and first grandchildren.

CHAPTER 7

What Pets Have Lived in the White House?

FACT: President James Buchanan gave his herd of elephants to a zoo!

Many first families have enjoyed pets. Over 400 animals have lived in the White House! There have been dogs, cats, ponies, and guinea pigs. But alligators, snakes, lions, and even elephants have lived at the White House, too! Pets have even had important jobs. Chelsea Clinton's cat Socks and the Bushes' dog Barney have hosted the White House Web site for children.

See You Later, Alligator!

Many important people visit the president. In 1826, the French Marquis de Lafayette visited President John Quincy Adams.

Lafayette brought an alligator as a gift for the president! The alligator lived in the East Room for two months. The snapping alligator surprised many White House visitors!

FACT:
Lafayette was a close friend of George Washington.

Whistling with President Jefferson

Dick, a mockingbird, was President Thomas Jefferson's favorite White House pet.

Dick perched on President Jefferson's shoulder while he worked. He whistled while President Jefferson played his violin.

Sometimes Dick even barked like a dog!

At night Dick hopped upstairs alongside President Jefferson. Do you think Dick sang President Jefferson to sleep?

FACT:
First Lady Dolley Madison had a talking parrot who entertained children visiting the White House.

Tad Lincoln's Racing Goats

Tad Lincoln had two goats named Nanny and Nanko. Tad hitched the goats to a cart so the goats could pull him around the White House.

One day Tad raced the goats through the White House. The goats upset a party Tad's mother, First Lady Mary Lincoln, was having. Mrs. Lincoln was angry. But she got even more angry when she heard President Lincoln laughing at the racing goats!

Teddy Roosevelt's White House Zoo

President Teddy Roosevelt and his family had more animals than any other first family. The Roosevelts had over fifty animals! Some of their animals lived at the White House. But the

FACT: Many presidents have summer homes.

Roosevelts had another home they called the "Summer White House." Many of the Roosevelts' animals lived at the Summer White House.

The Roosevelts had five bears, one lion, six guinea pigs, one pony, five snakes, two cats, one rat, five dogs, eight birds, one flying squirrel, one badger, one rabbit, eleven horses, one wildcat, one coyote, one pig, one kangaroo rat, and one lizard named Bill. Maybe they should have called their home the White Zoo!

CHAPTER 8

What Celebrations Are Held in the White House?

First families celebrate holidays, birthdays, anniversaries, and weddings at the White House. Many national celebrations are held at the White House every year.

Easter Egg Roll

Every Easter a special party called the Easter Egg Roll is held on the White House lawn. President Rutherford B. Hayes began this tradition in 1878. Back then children brought their own eggs to the Easter Egg Rolls. Today the White House provides the eggs.

The Easter Egg Roll is the largest public

celebration held at the White House. The president, first lady, first children, first grandchildren, and their pets all join thousands of visiting children to share the fun.

FACT: A human-size Easter Bunny comes to the Easter Egg Roll.

Egg croquet and egg catch were two games played at the first Easter Egg Rolls. In 1974 the popular egg-rolling race became a new tradition.

Children hold their eggs in spoons while they race across the lawn. Music, giant balloons, and, of course, an egg hunt are part of today's White House Easter celebrations.

First Weddings

In 1886 President Grover Cleveland married Frances Folsom in the White House. First Lady Frances Cleveland was the youngest first lady ever. She was only twenty-one years old when she became first lady! Their daughter Esther Cleveland was born in 1893. She was the first first child born in the White House.

FACT: There have been seventeen weddings at the White House.

Nine presidents' children have been married in the White House. The first was Maria Hester Monroe in 1820. She married her cousin, Samuel Lawrence, in the Blue Room.

John Quincy Adams was the only president's son to be married in the White House. He later became president.

The National Christmas Tree

Every holiday season the National Christmas Tree is lighted. The tree is placed somewhere on the White House lawn. There is a special ceremony with music and entertainment when the tree is lit. Fifty-six smaller trees are lighted on the "Pathway of Peace." There is a tree for each of the fifty states, our five territories, and the District of Columbia. In 1958 Alaska sent ten reindeer for the holiday celebration. The reindeer were part of the holiday scene in 1959, too.

FACT: A territory is land governed by the United States but isn't a state. Puerto Rico is a territory.

The National Tree tradition began in 1923. Almost every year since then a National Christmas Tree has been lighted. During World War II the tree was not lit for security reasons. In 2007 new energy-saving LED lights were first used.

Sometimes the president and the first lady invite special children to the White House to help light the National Christmas Tree.

First daughters Amy Carter and Chelsea Clinton helped light the tree, too. Every year thousands of people gather at the White House to watch the lighting of the National Christmas Tree. Millions more watch on TV.

FACT: In 1946 the lighting of the National Christmas tree was seen on TV for the first time.

You can write to the president at the White House. You might have to wait, but someone will answer your letter. The address is:

The White House
1600 Pennsylvania Avenue NW
Washington, D.C. 20500